# Teach Yourself Rock Bass.

*By David Gross.*

AMSCO

Photo credits
Technical photos: Barry Wetcher
page 4: Wide World Photos
page 22: MCA Records
page 27: Mark MacLaren
page 34: Atlantic Records
page 43: The Photo Reserve/Bill Sosin

Cover design by Pearce Marchbank
Series editor: Mark Michaels

e d c b

Distributed throughout the world by Music Sales Corporation:

799 Broadway, N.Y. 10003, New York, U.S.A.
78 Newman Street, London W1
27 Clarendon Street, Artarmon, Sydney NSW
Kölner Strasse 199, 5000 Cologne 90

Printed and Bound in England by J.B. Offset (Marks Tey) Ltd.
Station Approach, Marks Tey, Colchester, Essex.

# Contents

Introduction 4

Rudiments of Music 5

    Tablature 5
    Standard Notation 6
    Time 6
    Pitch 7
    $\frac{4}{4}$ Time 8

How to Hold the Electric Bass 9

Rock Rhythms 10

    Rock Styles 16
    Rests and Ties 18
    Review 21

Scales and Progressions 23

    Blues Progressions 23
    Twelve-Bar Blues Progressions 24
    Scales 29

Key Signatures 30
Transposing 35
More Progressions 40
Tone 42

Chords and Arpeggios 44

    Major Triads 44
    Minor Triads 48

Creating Your Own Bass Lines 53

Playing in a Group 57

Selecting Equipment 60

    Electric Bass 60
    Amplifier 60
    Effect Boxes 61
    Strings 61

Discography 62

# Introduction

If you are already playing rock bass and find that, even though you're playing the right notes, it just doesn't sound like it does on the record, then this book is for you. Step by step, I've presented the basic principles of music: harmony, melody, and especially rhythm, the key to really great bass playing. Learning about scales, chords and chord progressions will give you a real *feel* for playing the music as it increases your understanding of music's many dimensions. Soon you'll be able to develop solid bass lines in your own personal style, making it easy to jam with friends or actually play in a working band.

Throughout the text, all the exercises are presented in both standard notation and tablature. Whether or not you read music, you can follow the examples—and perhaps learn to read as you're playing. Reading standard notation is a valuable skill that's indispensable to the professional musician.

Remember: the bass is the true foundation of a rock group. Its rhythmic patterns often support the entire band. I have therefore stressed timing and phrasing, although the melodic aspects of rock bass are fully explored as well. Be sure to practice consistently; use a metronome, playing slowly at first, then gradually increasing the tempo. If you follow the examples in the book and practice regularly, your progress will be rapid and satisfying. It all takes time, but the reward is dynamite rock and roll!

**Rick Danko and** *The Band*

# Rudiments of Music

## Tablature

Two methods of writing music are used in this book; *tablature* and *standard notation*. The bass has four strings (E,A,D,G); the tablature system used in this book has four lines:

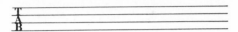

*Bar lines* divide the *staff* into *measures*:

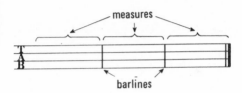

Each of the four lines of the tablature system represents a bass string. The top line stands for the highest-pitched string, the G string, the second line stands for the D string, the third line stands for the A string, and the bottom line stands for the lowest-pitched string, the E string:

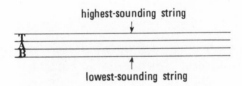

An 0 on the tablature staff indicates that you play that particular string open or unfretted. For example, an 0 on the bottom line means that you play the lowest-pitched string, E, open.

A number on the staff indicates the specific string and the fret position to play. A 5 on the bottom line indicates that you play the lowest string fretted on the fifth fret.

5

## Standard Notion

Music is generally written on the lines and in the spaces of a five-lined system called the *staff*.

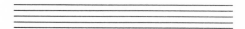

The lines and spaces of the staff do not represent specific notes until a particular *clef* is added. Music written for the electric bass uses the bass or F clef. It looks like this and must be written on every line of music.

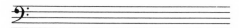

When notes go above or below the staff they are written on *leger lines*.

## Time

A *whole note* ( ○ ) receives four beats or counts, a *half note* ( ♩ ) receives two beats, and a *quarter note* ( ♩ ) gets one beat. The quarter note may be divided into smaller fractions. The chart below will help to explain the relationship between these different notes.

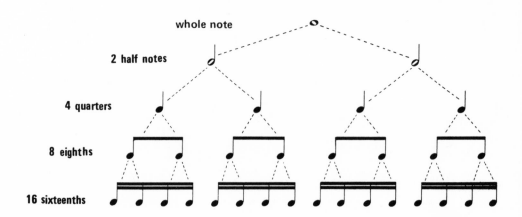

# Pitch

Every note has a neighboring note higher than it and one lower. To express this concept in musical notation we need to introduce two new ideas: The *sharp* (♯) and the *flat* (♭).

The sharp symbol preceding a note raises that note by one *half-step* or one fret. The flat symbol lowers a note by one half-step or fret. Now we can write a series of notes. In the first example all of the new notes are indicated by sharps; in the second, all of the new notes are indicated by flats. As you look at both of these examples, find each note on the bass. Just follow the indicated string.

Notice that whether notated in sharps or flats, both series of notes are the same. With the exception of the intervals E-F and B-C, the sharp of a note equals the flat of its alphabetical upper neighbor. Notes with this relationship—for example, A♯ and B♭, or C♯ and D♭—are called *enharmonic* equivalents.

# $\frac{4}{4}$ Time

All of the excercises in this book are written in $\frac{4}{4}$ or common time. The symbol for this is either $\frac{4}{4}$ or a **C** written on the staff, right after the clef ( **𝄢** ) symbol. $\frac{4}{4}$ time means that each bar or measure of music contains four quarter notes, each one receiving one beat. Therefore, each measure of music receives four beats. An eighth note gets half of one beat. When you are counting out a measure which contains a combination of quarter notes and eighth notes, count "1 and 2 and 3 and 4 and"; if it contains only quarter notes, just count "1 2 3 4." This way of counting will make it easier for you to find out on which beat the written note is to be played. For example:

The first passage contains "even eighth notes"—8 eighth notes to the measure. The second contains a combination of eighth and quarter notes in the following pattern: quarter, eighth, quarter, eighth, eighth, eighth. The number of beats which each of these notes receives is: one, one-half, one, one-half, one-half, one-half. Most rock music is written in $\frac{4}{4}$ time, which is why we will only be concerned with $\frac{4}{4}$ time in this book.

# How to Hold the Electric Bass

Before you begin playing the music in this book, study the following pictures. They show you the correct way to hold the bass, use a pick, use your fingers, and hold your left hand. Soon you'll get the feel of the instrument.

How to hold the bass.

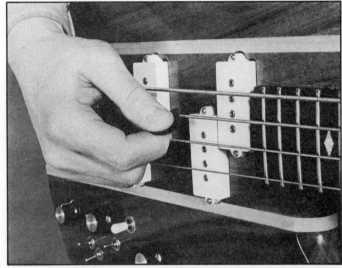
How to use a pick.

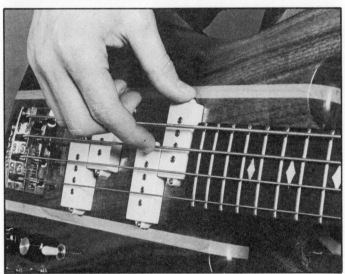
How to use your fingers.

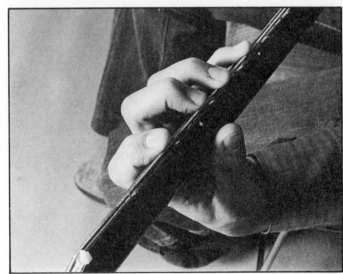
How to hold your left hand.

# Rock Rhythms

Rock music has always been a very rhythmic musical form; this makes the bass player particularly essential. A bassist's feel, sense of time, and drive really push the music. You therefore gain control over the dynamics and tension of the music.

This chapter deals specifically with rhythm. You will find that the driving power of groups like *Deep Purple*, *The Who*, *Wings* and *Queen* comes from the pulse given by the bass player.

To begin to gain rhythmic control of the music, start with your own record collection. Put on some of your favorite records and pay strict attention to what the bass and drummer are doing. Once you can listen and catch the phrasing your playing will noticeably improve.

Rhythm is based on note *durations*; as such it is distinct from the pitch value of the notes. Getting the right beat is as important as hitting the right notes.

This chapter is for you to familiarize yourself with various rhythms. Put your bass aside for the time being. Our emphasis is on first feeling the rhythms, then transferring them to the bass.

Here are some examples: Grab a pencil and tap out this rhythm:

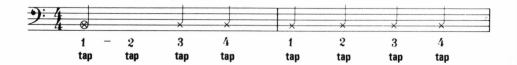

Now pick any note that comes into your head and sing it in the following rhythm:

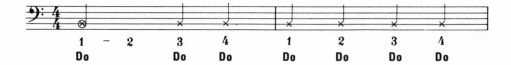

By doing this, and then doing the exercises on the following pages, you will begin to gain a good sense of time; by seeing the rock rhythms as you hear them, you'll find that reading the notes will become much easier.

Remember, start slowly and increase your tempos gradually. Use your foot to tap 1-2-3-4 in conjunction with your metronome. All the exercises are in $\frac{4}{4}$ time. Make sure you feel the tempo first, and let the metronome run a bit before you begin tapping.

Here are some easy rhythm patterns for you to sing and tap. They all use whole (○), half (𝅗𝅥), and quarter notes (♩).

Now pick up your bass. Let's use these same rhythm patterns and add some notes to them. You'll now be playing these notes instead of singing and tapping.

Play these next exercises slowly at first; use a metronome to make sure your tempo is correct. As you get the rhythm, you can speed it up.

12

When practicing, I find it best to expend no more than 45 to 50 minutes on serious concentration, and then take a break. Four hours of continuous practice does not necessarily mean four hours of learning. Take your time. If you are diligent, it will pay off.

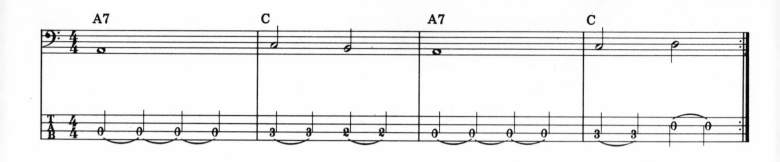

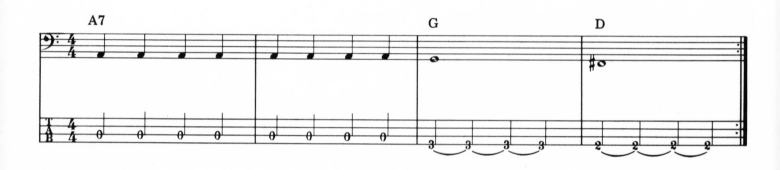

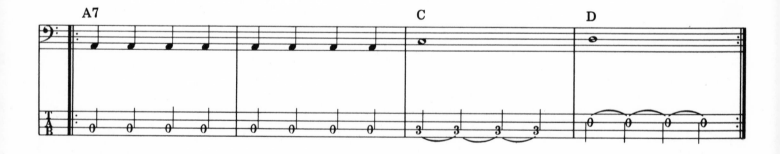

Here we have some more rhythm patterns that are to be sung and tapped. These patterns will incorporate eighth notes, which are used frequently in rock music.

You've probably noticed that some of these rhythms remind you of patterns you hear on records. After you play these patterns at a slow tempo make a point of increasing your speed, keeping in mind that this is rock music and should be played with that "rock feel" you hear every day.

## Rock Styles

At this point we should begin to talk about the different styles of rock bass playing. One style, exemplified by Paul McCartney of *Beatles* and *Wings* fame, is melodic with a driving pulse. Another, characterized by Andy Fraser of *Free*, is simpler and more rhythmic. A third style, which brought Jack Bruce to popularity, utilizes a lot of notes to offset the lead guitar and keep a driving beat.

With all these different styles it is difficult to choose just one. The best approach is to incorporate a little of each, plus what you yourself feel the music calls for. The next pattern presents a more melodic approach to bass playing.

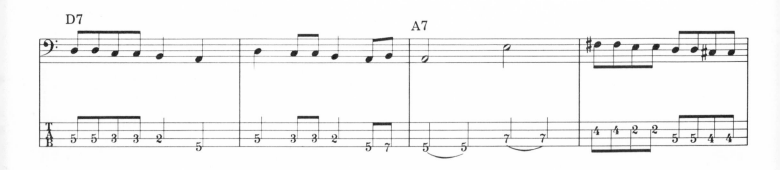

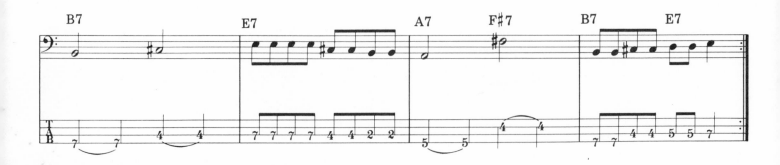

Here are a few lines in the simpler rhythmic style:

## Rests and Ties

Here are some more eighth-note patterns. These incorporate *rests* and *ties*. A rest is a pause in the music, with a time value just like a note. The four types of rests that we will be concerned with are:

whole rest        half rest        quarter rest        eighth rest

Notice when you listen to records that there are times when it seems the bass is not playing (laying out) or is hanging on one note. For example, this happens in the *Beatles'* song "Something" or "Dandelion" by the *Rolling Stones*. What the bass player is doing is creating space. Being at the front line of the rhythm section, the bass, by playing less, is keeping both the harmonic and rhythmic aspects of the song more interesting.

These patterns are for singing and tapping:

These next patterns deal with *syncopation*. Syncopation occurs when you break up a musical phrase with a rest or tie. A tie is shown as a curved line connecting a note and its repetition; it means that the two notes should be played as one, with the combined time value of the two tied notes. Syncopation creates movement in the music and gives the lead instrument more room to improvise.

(rest on downbeat)                              tied notes

As a rock bass player your job is best done when you can create excitement without stepping on any of the other musicians' toes.

The following patterns are for singing and tapping:

Now pick up your bass and play the next few pages of excercises. As you practice these rhythms, you will find it easier to play these same patterns faster; in doing so, concentrate on making certain that you are holding each note for its actual time value.

## Review

If you have followed these exercises through, you now have a solid knowledge of basic reading and rhythmic skills. Keep in mind that the rock bass player's primary function is to keep the tempo steady, and to interact well with the other players.

The next chapter deals with the blues progressions that account for most of what you hear today in contemporary music. Before you continue, play the following exercises; try to remember all we have discussed. Sounds good, doesn't it?

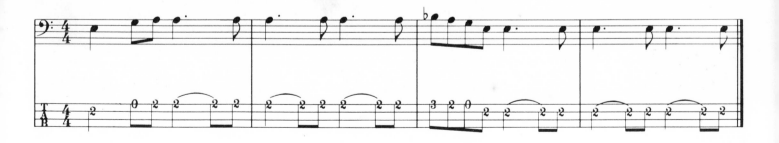

John Entwistle

# Scales and Progressions

## Blues Progressions

Blues patterns make up a great deal of the basic *progressions* used in rock music. A progression is a sequence of chords which makes up a musical phrase.

The blues is a contemporary style of vocal and instrumental music, introduced into this country when African slaves were brought to the United States in the 1800s. Blues grew out of their work songs and gospel spirituals. The first traceable example of the blues was written in 1909 and published in 1912 by W. C. Handy, a black blues artist living at that time. It was called the "Memphis Blues."

A great many blues artists were active in the early and middle 1900s, making the blues a happening musical form. Artists like Big Bill Broonzy, Son House, Blind Lemon Jefferson, B. B. King and Albert King are just a few of the great blues musicians who have brought us this great music.

The blues gave birth to rock and roll in the 1950s. People like Bo Diddley, Little Richard, Chuck Berry and Elvis Presley brought blues-based music to a larger audience. Current artists with roots in the blues tradition include the *Rolling Stones, J. Geils Band, Foghat, Savoy Brown* and the *Climax Blues Band.*

In this chapter I will give you the basics for playing the blues. Here are some simple riffs to get you started. Keep in mind that these phrases should be played slowly at first; concentrate on good time and a clear, even tone.

# Twelve-Bar Blues Progressions

Play this exercise; listen carefully to its rhythmic pattern:

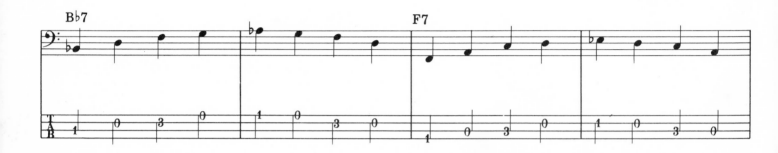

What you have just played is a *twelve-bar blues progression*. It is called that because if you count the number of bars (measures) you will find twelve of them. The bass line is called a *walking bass line* because the bass plays on every beat of the measure, creating a "walking" feel. This pattern is often heard in recordings by Fats Domino, Chuck Berry and Little Richard, and is still popular today. All twelve-bar blues progressions do not necessarily have walking bass lines.

The next group of patterns will take you through some ascending (going higher in pitch) and descending (going lower in pitch) progressions. Bass lines are meant to create moods; by playing lines that travel up and down you will assume a more active part in the music. These patterns should be played very deliberately to insure that you understand the concept of ascending and descending lines.

If you are going to use a pick, like Felix Pappilardi (of *Mountain*) or Paul McCartney, it is best to acquire a few hard and a few medium picks and choose the ones best suited for yourself. Soft picks give an indistinct sound and they break very easily. The clean attack a pick provides is widely used today in a variety of situations, but the famous "pop" that you get with your fingers is just as valuable. The pop can be heard on "Lowdown" by Boz Scaggs, on George Harrison's *33 1/3*, or by Lee Sklar on the latest James Taylor album, *JT*. Playing with your fingers will also give you a more rounded or "fat" tone, whereas a pick produces more of a click-type or trebly sound.

Learning to use both a pick and your fingers will lead you to become a more versatile bassist. It never hurts to know more than one way of doing something.

Here are two more progressions to play:

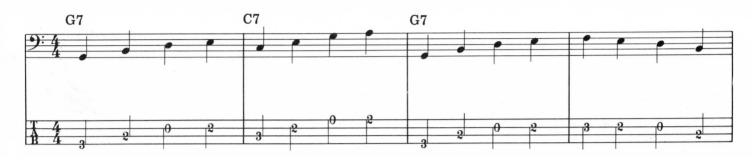

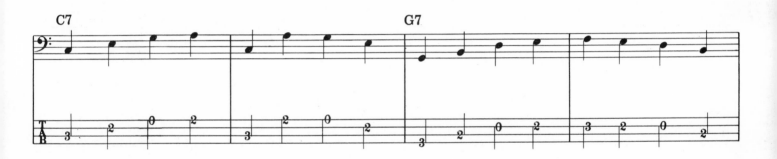

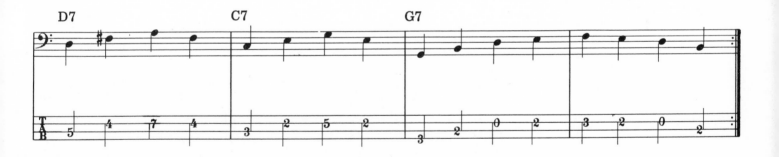

As you can see in these two progressions, the lines go up and down, creating movement in the music. The *number* of notes that is being played is not as important as the fact that the bass line can stand alone as a pure and simple melody which, when added to the lead melody, supports the whole group.

The next pattern uses *octaves* as a means of emphasizing the basic notes. Instead of just plucking the A note on an A chord the line uses both the low A note and the A an octave (eights steps) above. This helps to support the rhythm section without getting in the way of the vocals or the soloist.

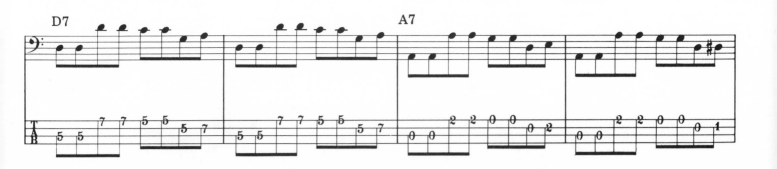

John Tout of *Renaissance*

This progression is a shuffle. It lies on the same note but, by using eighth-note patterns, the music is pushed to create a driving blues.

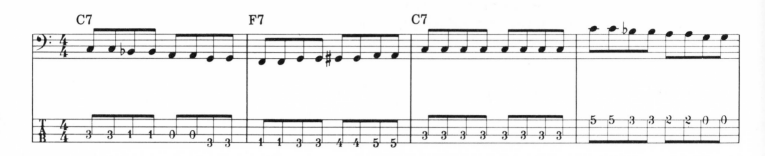

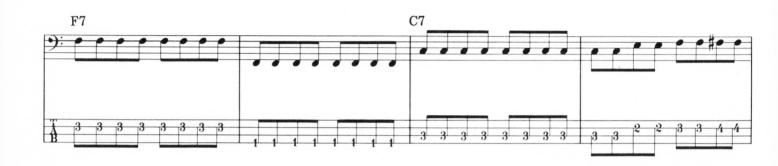

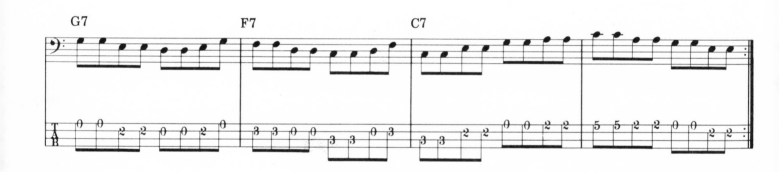

# Scales

As well as being twelve-bar blues progressions, these patterns have another name: *I-IV-V* progressions. The Roman numerals correspond to the degrees of the scale. This is an F major scale:

A *scale* is a succession of eight notes arranged in a pattern of whole steps and half steps. Referring to the degrees of the scale, you can see that the I is an F note, the IV is Bb and the V is C. With this system you'll be able to play a I-IV-V progression anywhere on the bass, in any key.

There are twelve tones in western music, each a half step away from the other. Starting from C, these twelve tones are:

C, C#/Db, D, D#/Eb, E, F, F#/Gb, G, G#/Ab, A, A#/Bb, B, C

With the exception of the intervals from E to F and B to C (*half-steps*), all the intervals between *naturals* (notes neither sharped nor flatted) are *whole steps*. This arrangement of whole steps and half steps (from C to C) is a *major scale*. The pattern of intervals for a major scale is always the same, no matter what key you're playing in.

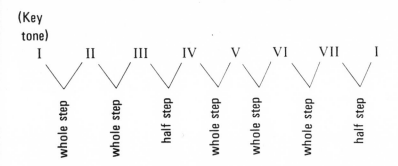

With the above information you can construct a major scale in *any* key. For instance, in the key of A, start with the key note, move up a whole step, another whole step and so on, applying the pattern, and you'll end up with an A major scale.

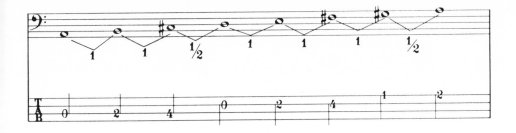

## Key Signatures

Almost all music is written in a particular *key*. The key refers to the scale associated with the *key tone* (or *tonic*), the note on which the piece of music often begins and usually ends. The key is indicated by the *key signature,* which appears between the clef sign and the time signature (in this book, $\frac{4}{4}$ ). The key signature is made up of the sharps and flats in the scale of that key. For example, F major has one flat—B♭. So the key of F major is indicated by a flat sign on the B line of the staff:

Note that the key of C major contains *no* sharps or flats:

To cancel a sharp or a flat at any point in the music, a **natural sign** ( ♮ ) is used. For example, if we were playing in the key of F major:

the ♮ would cancel the ♭ and make the note a B natural. The natural sign only applies to the measure it is used in, and must be notated later if it is to be used again.

Before you begin to play any piece of music, check the key signature so you will know which notes (if any) are to be sharped or flatted whenever they occur.

Here is a list of the major key signatures. You should memorize the names of the sharps and flats for each of the keys, especially the ones that we will cover in this book. Here are the ones primarily used in today's rock.

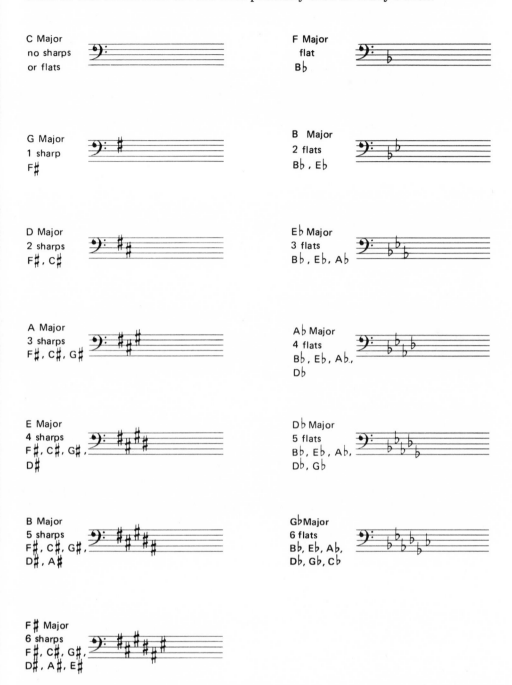

C Major
no sharps
or flats

F Major
flat
B♭

G Major
1 sharp
F♯

B Major
2 flats
B♭, E♭

D Major
2 sharps
F♯, C♯

E♭ Major
3 flats
B♭, E♭, A♭

A Major
3 sharps
F♯, C♯, G♯

A♭ Major
4 flats
B♭, E♭, A♭, D♭

E Major
4 sharps
F♯, C♯, G♯, D♯

D♭ Major
5 flats
B♭, E♭, A♭, D♭, G♭

B Major
5 sharps
F♯, C♯, G♯, D♯, A♯

G♭ Major
6 flats
B♭, E♭, A♭, D♭, G♭, C♭

F♯ Major
6 sharps
F♯, C♯, G♯, D♯, A♯, E♯

Let's get back to the blues progressions we were talking about earlier in the chapter. There are a few more progressions in the I-IV-V pattern.

Again, a C major scale:

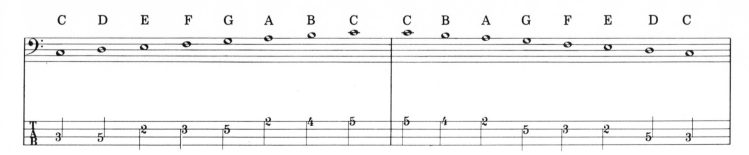

To find the I-IV-V progression we look at the scale: I is C, IV is F, and V is G. Below is a progression of the ascending-descending type. After you have played this progression at a slow tempo, experiment with your metronome at various settings. You will find the same notes take on a totally different character with each tempo change.

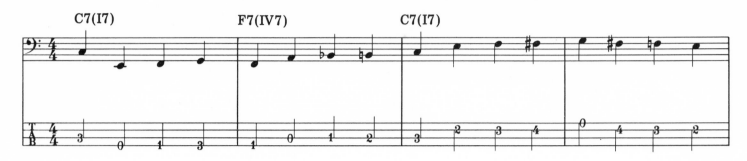

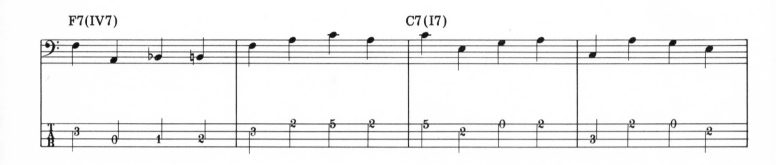

Certain one- or two-bar phrases can be used over and over again as a bass line to an entire song. (Jack Bruce on "Sunshine of Your Love," "My Girl" by the *Temptations* and "Manic Depression" by Jimi Hendrix, with Noel Redding on the bass.)

Here are a few phrases typifying that kind of line. Note that the music is in the key of E major.

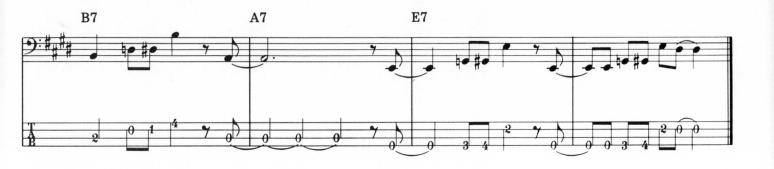

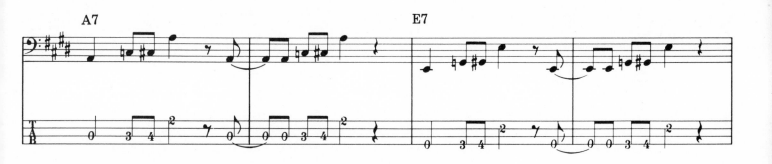

The next pattern is reminiscent of the riff used by *Ten Years After* in the standard blues "Good Mornin' Little Schoolgirl." It is a primarily eighth-note rhythm exercise which, when played loud, gives a driving sound to the music.

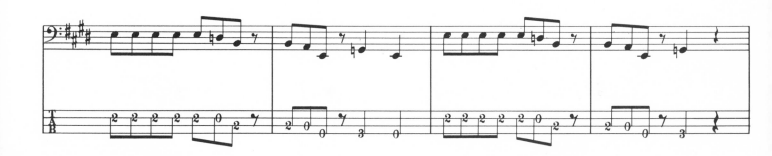

Chris Squire of *Yes*

# Transposing

When your fingers begin to memorize these patterns in the keys they are written in, it is time to begin playing them in other keys to familiarize yourself with the neck. This process is called *transposition*.

Let's take a riff in E major:

Now that you have played the riff in E major, let's play it in the key of A major. The trick in transposing is to remember the particular fingering and duplicate it in the new key.

By just moving the fingerings to other strings and up and down the neck, you can play any riff in any key.

Here is another simple riff in the key of G. Let's transpose this through five other keys:

**C Major**

**D Major**

**A Major**

**F Major**

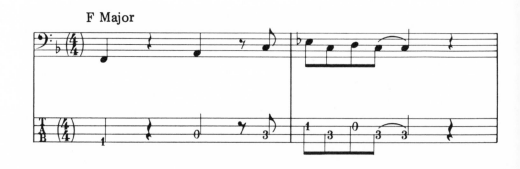

**Bb Major**

In the 50s, rock music was heavily influenced by the blues. This next pattern is similar to that played in a song called "Boney Maroney." It utilizes eighth-note patterns as well as a repeating phrase. Play it at a medium tempo. Again, note the key signature: the three sharps (C♯, F♯, G♯) mean A major.

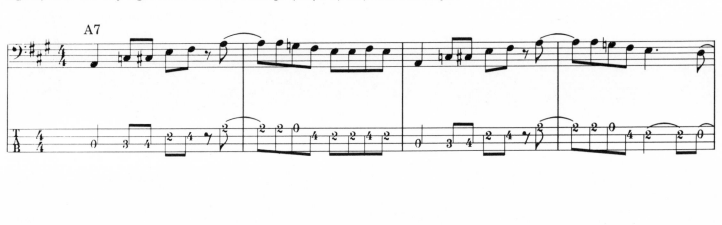

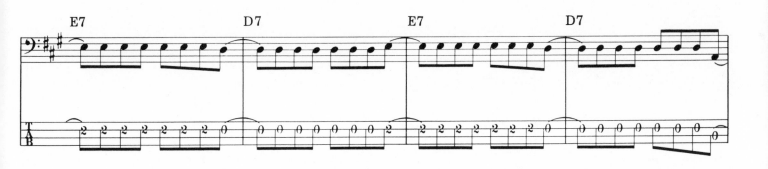

Here is another twelve-bar blues progression in the key of C. See how many keys you can take it through. I will start the progression for you in the five other most important keys in rock music. Practice this slowly to learn transposing thoroughly:

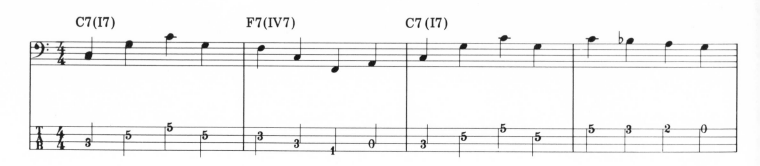

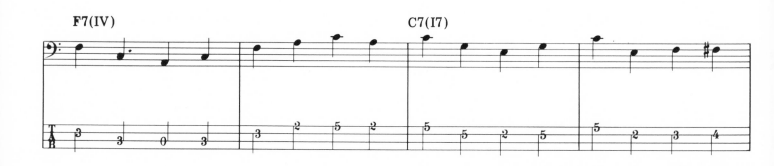

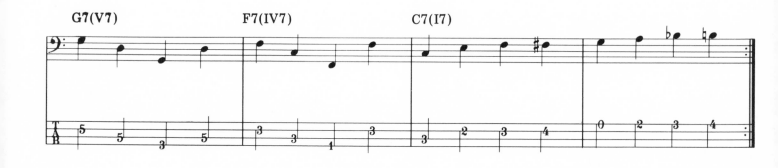

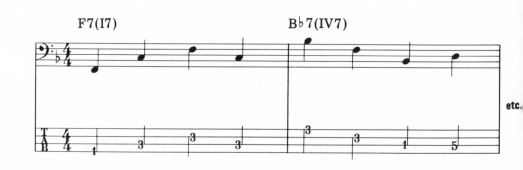

etc.

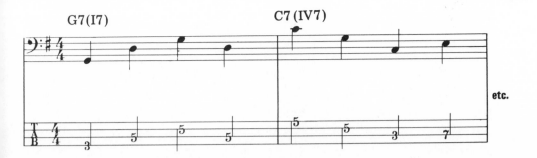

G7(I7)　　　　　　　　　C7 (IV7)

etc.

A7(I7)　　　　　　　　　D7(IV7)

etc.

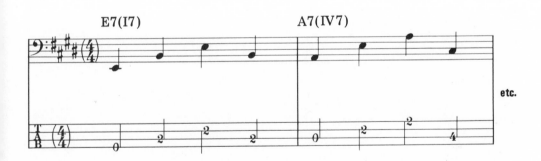

D7(I7)　　　　　　　　　G7(IV7)

etc.

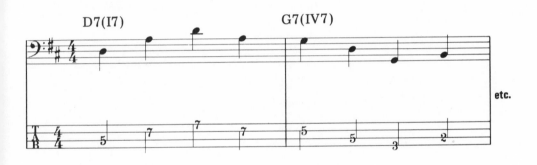

E7(I7)　　　　　　　　　A7(IV7)

etc.

# More Progressions

Blues are not confined to just the I-IV-V progression. Other progressions are frequently used in rock music; one in particular is the I-VI-II-V progression. This one was used a great deal in the 50s by groups like the *Dovells*, *Dion and the Belmonts*, the *Drifters* and many others.

This progression is built on the first, second, fifth and sixth notes of the major scale.

Here is an example using the C major scale.

We take the same steps to discover the notes of this progression as we did for the I-IV-V progression. First find the I (C), then the VI (A), then the II (D) and finally the V (G). Using this same formula, you can find any I-VI-II-V progression in any key.

This next exercise will take you through the six keys we have been working with using the I-VI-II-V progression. This pattern is reminiscent of the song "Silhouettes," a huge hit of the 50s which was recorded by *Herman's Hermits* in the 60s.

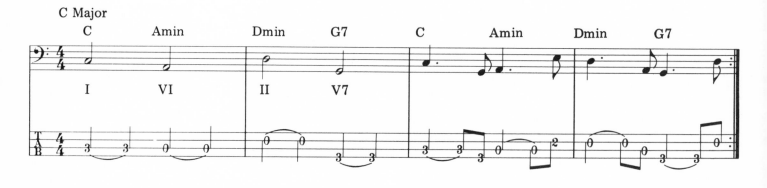

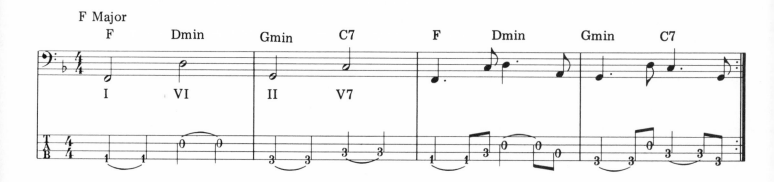

40

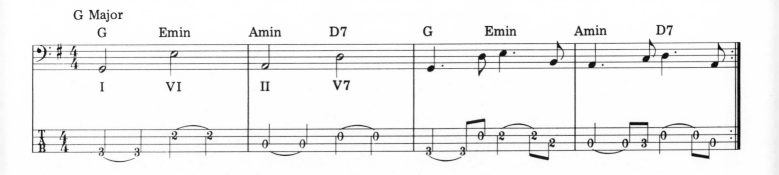

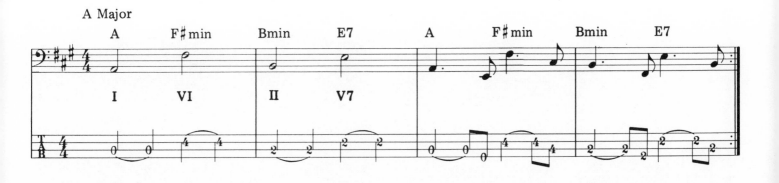

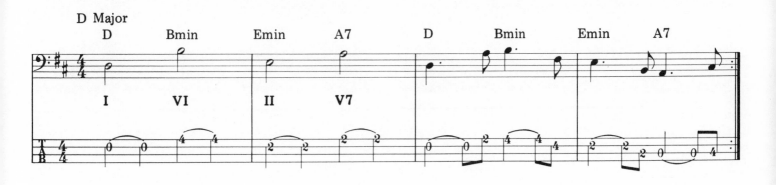

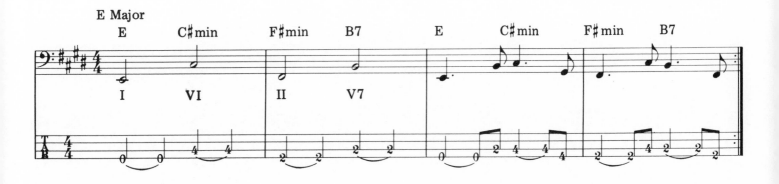

# Tone

At this point you should begin to think about the electric bass in terms of what tone you want to hear. For example, do you want to get a round, bassy sound, or a sharp trebly tone? Playing through the previous exercises at various tempos has developed your ability to move around on the instrument fairly well. Now it's time to put the music and the tone together.

We spoke about picks briefly on page 24 ; now let's talk about fingers. There are two basic ways to attack the strings. One is to hit the string on top, the other is to pluck the string from underneath (see figure below).

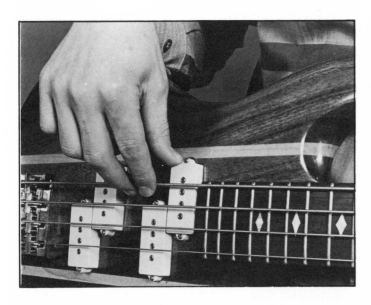 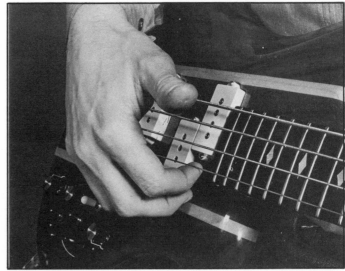

Practice both styles of attack; you'll soon be able to identify which type is used on your favorite records. Gradually you'll come to know which type is best suited to any particular music.

Some bass players who use this fingerstyle approach are Willie Weeks (George Harrison's *33 1/3*), David Hungate (Boz Scaggs' *Lowdown*), Lee Sklar (James Taylor's *JT*) and Larry Graham (of *Graham Central Station*).

Here are three progressions to get your right hand moving:

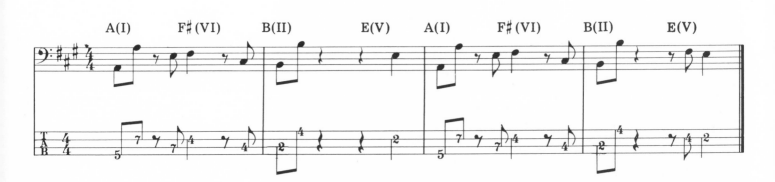

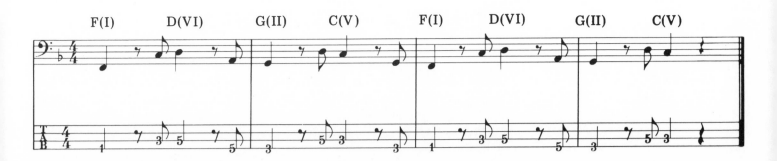

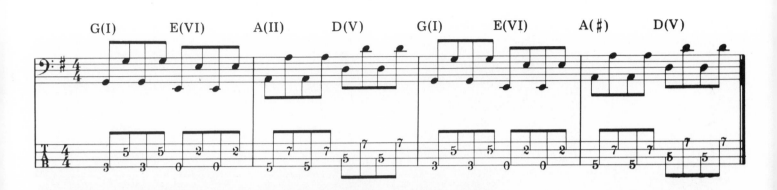

Paul McCartney

# Chords and Arpeggios

## Major Triads

This chapter deals primarily with chords—the harmonic part of music—and further explorations into rhythmic patterns.

You have been working in the six most frequently played keys in rock music. Since there are twelve keys in all, here are three more to familiarize yourself with.

**Eb Major**

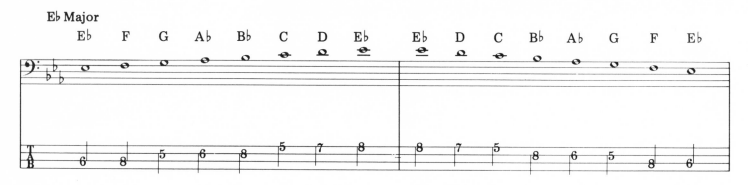

**Bb Major**

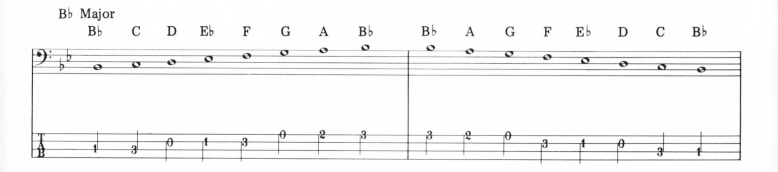

**B Major**

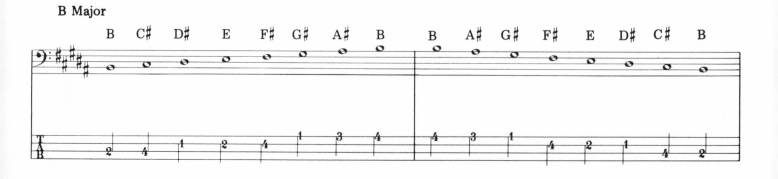

As you remember from **page 29** , a major scale is a series of eight notes arranged in a pattern of whole and half steps. Major chords are constructed from these scales. Let's take the Eb major scale and use its first, third and fifth notes, playing them over and over.

These three notes make up the Eb major triad. A *triad* is a chord consisting of three notes: the root, and its third and fifth.

Here is a rhythm pattern using the root, third and fifth of the Eb major scale.

This next exercise will take you through the other eight keys that we have been working in. This rhythm pattern should be practiced over and over until you are confident about it.

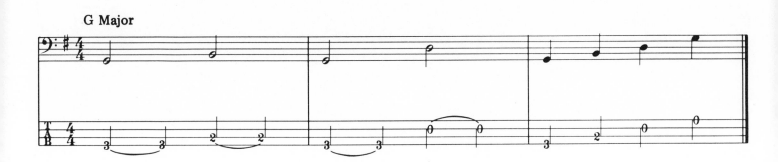

**A Major**

**D Major**

Learning these basic chord note patterns will help you when a player just calls out the chord changes to a song—and you have to play. Once you know the notes in a chord, adding other scale tones to create interesting bass lines will come easily.

For instance, play these chords:

**C Major**            **F Major**

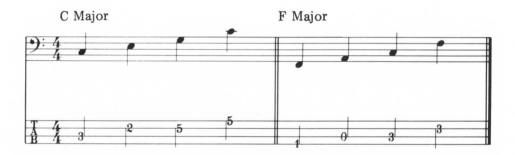

Now, add some interesting rhythmic variety to create a more interesting bass line:

**C Major**            **F Major**

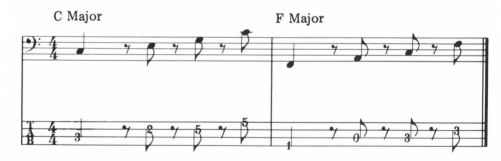

46

By adding a couple of notes from the appropriate scales you can have a better pattern rhythmically and melodically.

Here are the chord-note patterns which will aid in creating better bass lines. Try to memorize them.

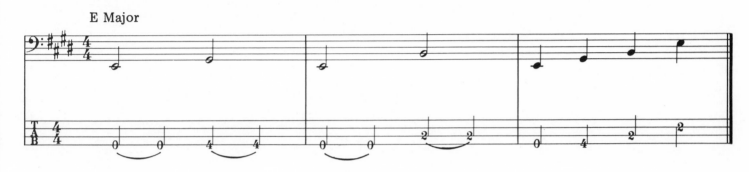

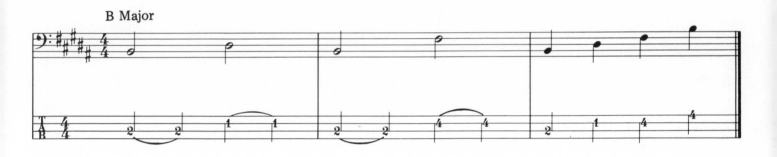

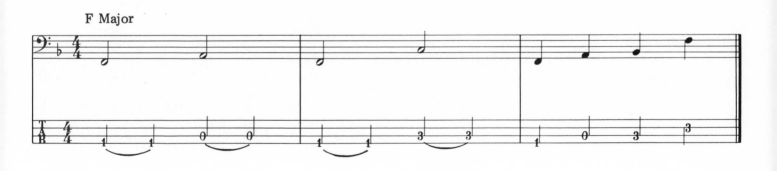

47

Bb Major

The major scale contains three major triads which are built on the first, fourth, and fifth note of the scale. Let's go back to the C major scale:

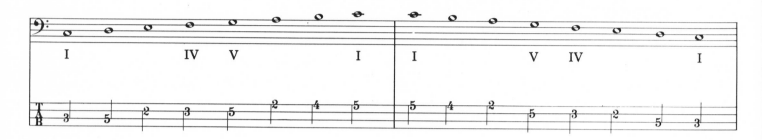

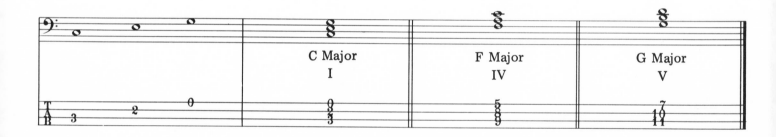

These three chords are the basis of the I-IV-V blues progression. But the bass does not usually play chords. Instead, by playing the notes of the triad one at a time, as in the previous rhythm exercises, you will have played what is called an arpeggio. An *arpeggio* is the playing of the tones of a chord one after another in succession, instead of playing them simultaneously.

## Minor Triads

The major scale also contains three minor triads, built on the second, third, and sixth degrees of the scale. A minor triad consists of the root ( first degree of the scale) with the third (which is flatted) and the fifth above it.

Here is the C major scale:

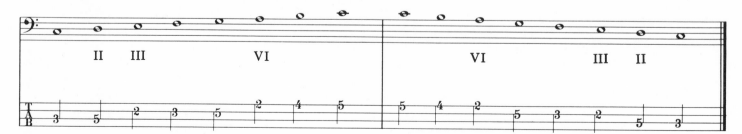

In a C major scale, the minor triads are built on D (II), E (III) and A (VI).

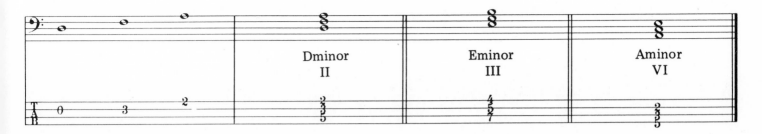

| | D minor<br>II | E minor<br>III | A minor<br>VI |

In the following example, you can see the difference between major and minor triads. In the C minor triad, the third is flatted. Similarly, an F minor triad contains an A♭ while the F major calls for an A natural.

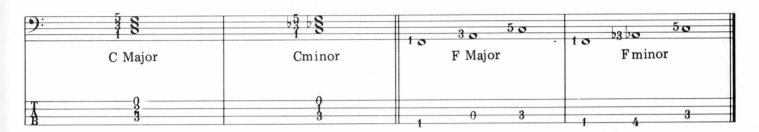

| C Major | C minor | F Major | F minor |

Here is a chart of the minor arpeggios in the eight keys we have been working in. As with the major arpeggios, practice these until you can play them confidently.

G minor

A minor

**D minor**

**E minor**

**B minor**

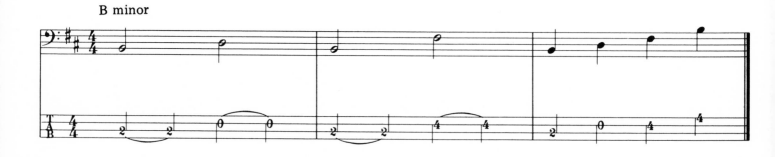

**F minor**

**B♭ minor**

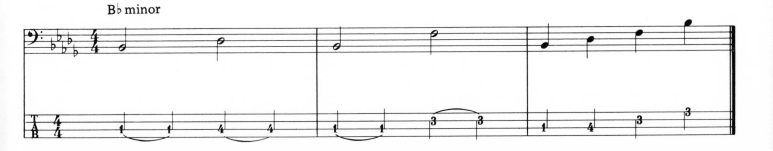

**E♭ minor**

Here is a chart of triads in a major scale using every note of the scale. Let's begin with C major:

**C Major**   **D minor**   **E minor**   **F Major**

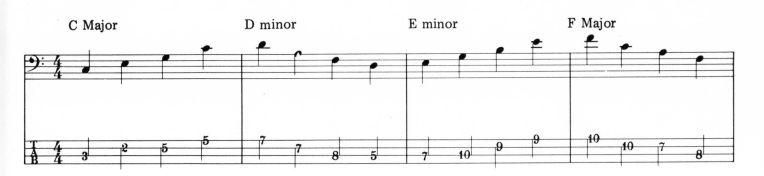

**G Major**   **A minor**   **B minor (♭5)**

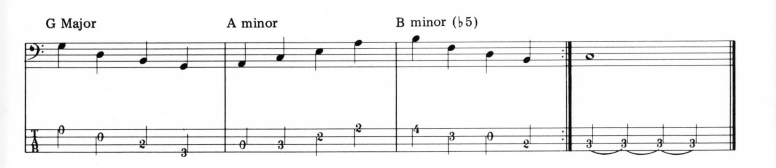

All chords are based on these major and minor triads, but there's a lot more you can do. For example, you can add the seventh of the scale to create more interesting chord sounds.

When you add these notes there are certain rules that apply. For instance, the major seventh chord is built 1 (root), 3,5,7. The minor seventh is built 1 (root),♭3,5,♭7. The fifth degree of the major scale is the only exception to this rule: it is built 1 (root), 3,5,♭7. This is a dominant seventh chord. The chord built on the seventh degree of the scale gives you a minor triad with the fifth flatted. Adding a seventh to the chord makes its construction 1 (root),♭3,♭5,♭7.

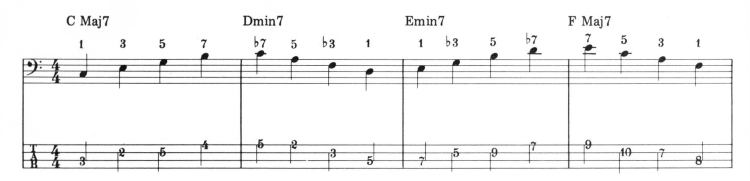

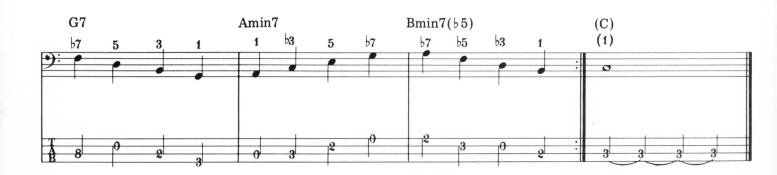

With this knowledge of how to build chords, it will be much easier to create your own bass lines from simple chord changes. The next chapter will deal with the creation of your own bass line. Remember, playing a bass line and just using arpeggios of chords are two entirely different things. Knowing the harmonic aspect is important, but being able to use your knowledge of chords to produce melody lines is really where it's at.

# Creating Your Own Bass Lines

You now have the basics which enable you to create your own bass lines by just looking at chord symbols. Rock bass playing can be a simple reaffirmation of the chords by just playing the root (first note of a chord) or it can be as complex as a melody line accompanying the lead instrument.

You should now have the technical knowledge, theoretical understanding and facility in playing quite a few rhythm styles to be able to play rock bass with other musicians. But what if you get together with a drummer, piano player, singer and lead guitarist, and they throw a chart of chord symbols at you? What do you do? How do you begin? This chapter will focus on the practical aspects of getting down and doing it.

Let's start with a set of chord changes and see what you can make of it.

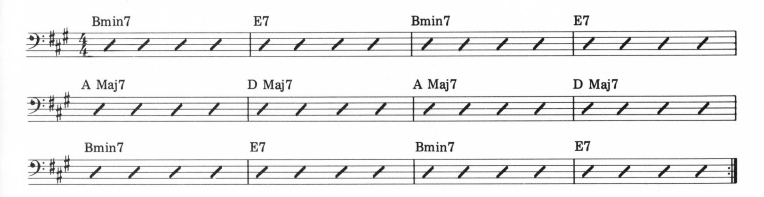

Play the note that corresponds to the chord name, four beats to a measure. Play four quarter notes on B in the bars that say B minor 7, play the E note for four quarters in the bars that say E7, play the A note for four, and the D note for four in their respective bars.

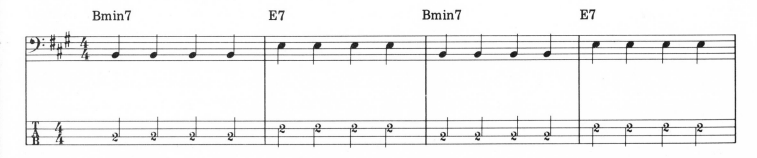

53

Next, alternate between the root and fifth of the chord (1-5-1-5 etc.). This will begin to add melodic interest to a harmonic bass line.

We are aiming for a bass line that both keeps the chord defined and adds some variety to it.

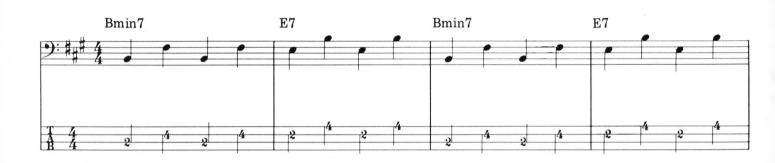

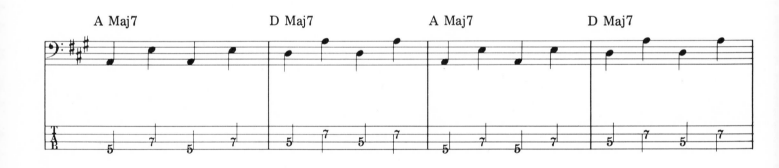

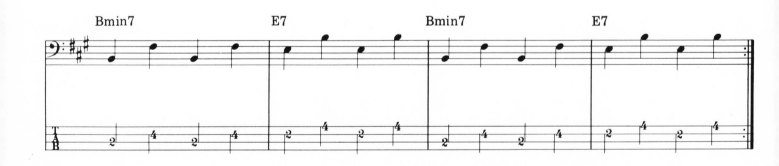

For certain songs the 1-5-1-5 type of bass line is all that is necessary for the tune. Groups like the *Eagles, Doobie Brothers, Firefall* and some of the country rock groups all utilize the 1-5-1-5 lines in some of their songs. However, with the more progressive groups like *Queen, The Who, Be-Bop Deluxe, Genesis* and others, that particular pattern is not enough. Let's use the formula for arpeggios in the next chart. Keep in mind that you are keeping time evenly as well as hitting the notes distinctly.

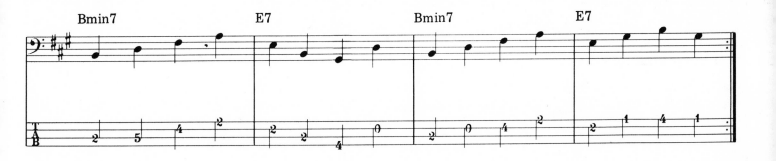

Once you have the tune worked out harmonically (chords) and have given some melodic activity to the piece (arpeggios), it would be wise to add some rhythmic variety as well. Rhythmic variety does not mean playing lots of notes; it could very well be the subtraction of notes that makes the song interesting. Using this progression, here's an example of rhythmic variety.

Let's review these techniques. We've gone from playing just the root, to the 1-5-1-5 line, to adding arpeggios, to rhythmic variations. Once you have this pattern down, your bass lines will come fluently. Now you can add specific variations based on your own feelings and understanding of the music. Don't be afraid to experiment, to put your own personality into the bass line. The basic pattern will always assure a correct bass line; the addition of your own style guarantees that the sound coming out of the amp is not just what's on the sheet music, but has your personal signature. Remember that whatever you try, the three dimensions to always keep in mind are harmony, melody and rhythm.

# Playing in a Group

Now that you've gotten this much together, you should begin playing with other musicians and maybe even forming your own group. The most important thing to remember is that it takes time to get familiar with other players, and for the result to sound like music. Practice and patience are most necessary.

To start with, you and the drummer must get in sync. This means you should listen to what is being done with the bass drum and try to follow it with your own bass line. Next listen to what the drummer is doing with his hi-hat. The drummer could be playing quarter notes on the hi-hat:

This should make your pattern fall on the one and the three of the measure to strengthen the time:

Sometimes he might be playing a simple eighth-note pattern on the hi-hat:

So it would be best for you to play a busier line:

When you start to play songs that you hear on the radio, *listen* to the parts you are going to play and take it from there. A critical listener can hear the bass and drums playing together and then apply this unity to his or her own band.

In another situation which often occurs, a chart is thrown in front of you and you have to read it as well as interpret what you and the drummer should be doing to make the music cook. For example, take this blues progression:

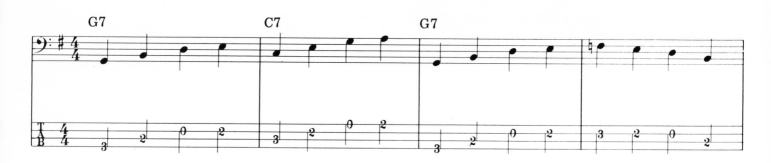

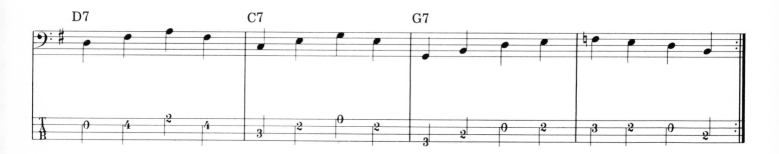

After you have read this, keep in mind that the drummer, knowing it is a blues tune, will play either with a shuffle feel like "I'm a Man" by the *Yardbirds*, or a funky blues like "Let Me Love You" by the *Jeff Beck Group* or in a rock and roll style like the early *Rolling Stones*. This makes it easier for you the bassist, to blend in, since his pattern will set up how you play your line. Always listen for the downbeat, and try to feel the drummer and concentrate on the written music simultaneously.

After hooking in with a drummer, it becomes necessary to add a guitar to the line-up for solos and support. Adding a guitar means that you now have to listen to two people and interact favorably with the music. Since the guitarist will add both rhythmic and melodic support to the tune, you have to be aware of his line and make sure that yours does not interfere. Too much playing can conflict with the musical ideas.

The simple rule to follow is: when the guitar is soloing, leave room in your line for his contribution, but when he is playing rhythm, you have the freedom to play a little more.

As the three of you practice your parts, it's soon time to add a second guitar or a piano. Acquiring another melodic instrument requires you to decide how to create a line which is pleasing to both the listener and the players but which doesn't conflict with any of them. This can be done by playing a bit more on the chord tones as discussed in the chapter on blues progressions, and occasionally playing a fill.

When your band is complete, *dynamics* can be added to the piece. Dynamics add expression to a piece of music. When you play loudly in a certain part of the song or softly in another, you are creating dynamic levels.

When you're playing a blues progression, a good dynamic change is to lower your volume at the start of a solo and build up volume and intensity as the soloist starts cooking. Another technique is to have the bass and drums play through the progression without the other instruments. This works great when you have already had a couple of solos and you want to grab the audience and then burst into another flurry of solos.

If you have a singer who is taking charge as the leader of the band, it's necessary to keep an eye on him or her for counting of the songs and signaling the endings. Also, when a singer is in the middle of a verse, it is best for the bass and drums to be playing simple patterns, so as not to take away from the lyrics being sung.

Remember that when you are playing in a group, the key is to play together and develop a sound that is more than just four or five people playing at the same time. It is more important to have a true band sound than to be merely a group of soloing musicians playing together. It does take time.

Play a lot with your group and continue to practice alone, and you will be surprised at the progress that you will make.

# Selecting Equipment

## Electric Bass

At this time there are a great many electric basses on the market. With the advance of electronic technology, basses are becoming quite versatile in the sounds they can create. Despite all the added accessories that are available, the standard of the industry is still the **Fender Precision Bass**. It has one pickup that is split in half, one volume and one tone knob. Fender also makes a **Jazz Bass** model that utilizes two pickups, a volume and two tone controls. It has a slimmer neck and is useful if you have small hands. Another Fender is the **Telecaster Bass**, which also uses one pickup but has a thinner neck than the Precision. Fender also makes two three-quarter size electric basses, which have smaller necks and bodies—the Mustang and the Musicmaster.

The **Gibson** company has come out with several models that are in use today, including the **EBO, EB3**, the **Grabber**, and the **Ripper**. The EBO and EB3 have a smaller neck than the Fenders and use either one or two pickups. The Grabber and the Ripper have longer necks (comparable to Fender) and use either a sliding pickup or two mounted pickups. The sound they produce is rounder than the Fender, which has a punchy type of sound.

The **Rickenbacker** company has a line of bass guitars that are very popular with Paul McCartney and groups like *Yes*, and *Genesis*. They can be purchased in either mono or stereo versions and they can produce a very trebly tone.

**Rickenbacker**

**C. B. Rich**

Many smaller companies have come out with electric basses: **Travis Bean** (their basses have aluminum necks and two pickups); **Alembic** (their basses are very expensive but have features no other bass has—pre-amps built in, long-scale necks, etc.); and **Carl Thompson** (who custom makes fretted and fretless basses that have wonderful tones). Ernie Ball, the string manufacturer, has a nonelectric bass shaped like an overgrown acoustic guitar called the Earthwood bass. The author uses a custom-made C. B. Rich bass for performing and studio work. The list goes on, with new manufacturers coming out with new styles and electronic gizmos all the time.

The important thing is to find a bass that suits you and your needs. Try as many as you like, making sure that the frets are all in tune and the same height, the neck is straight, and all the electronics are working properly.

## Amplifier

For the beginner, a large amplifier is simply not necessary. **Ampeg Electronics** puts out an amp called the **B-15**, which is used professionally both in studios and on live dates at small clubs. It is quite dependable, and earns its nickname, "the workhorse." Other small amps are made by **Peavey (TNT)**, **Fender (Bassman)**, **Sunn**, and **Acoustic**.

If you are playing in a group that uses big amplification, check out **Gallien Kruger, Ampeg SVT, Sunn Coliseum**, and **Acoustic 360** amps.

As with basses, try as many as it takes till you feel comfortable with one.

# Effect Boxes

After you have been playing your bass awhile, you might like to experiment with a couple of effect boxes to enhance your sound. Many different companies make these boxes, or **pedals**; I will describe the function of each and you can decide which box fills your particular need. Once again it is important to try as many as you can to be sure you get exactly what you want. A few of the bigger companies making them are **MXR, Electroharmonix, Vox, Morley, Dan Armstrong**, and **S. Hawk**.

A "wah wah" pedal does exactly that – creates a tonal effect of going from bassy to trebly producing that wah wah type of sound.

Phase shifters give the bass a swooshing sound similar to that used by organists through a Leslie speaker. Try many of these, because some function better for guitar. You need one that can reproduce the low E string cleanly. A flanger is a more sophisticated phase shifter and should be more effective on the low E string. Once again, check out a few.

A funk machine gives a wah effect with extra punch, but can not be regulated as easily because it has no pedal. It is used a lot by Larry Graham of *Graham Central Station* and by Will Lee of the *Brecker Brothers*.

These and other effect boxes should be available at your local music store. If they don't have a particular model, I'm sure it can be ordered.

Wah-wah and fuzz pedal

Phase shifter

# Strings

Strings are made in three different styles; flatwound, roundwound, and half round (a combination of the two). I suggest you try out a few sets to find which suits you best. The roundwound are hardest on the fingers and the neck of the bass, but produce a very clean, trebly tone; the flatwound have a rounder sound and are easy on the hands. A few of the major companies producing strings are **Fender, Rotosound** (John Entwistle uses these), **La Bella, D'Addario**, and **Dean Markley**. These strings come in light, medium, and heavy gauges. Your best bet is to start with medium-gauge strings and take it from there, trying others as the need or desire arises.

# Discography

**Jack Bruce**

The bassist for Cream. He created a style that features a lot of melody. *Fresh Cream*, RSO 3009; *Disreali Gears*, RSO 3010; *Wheels of Fire*, 2-RSO 3802.

**Jack Cassidy**

Played with the Jefferson Airplane and then formed his own band, Hot Tuna. He has a very blues-oriented style. *Surrealistic Pillow*, RCA 3766; *After Bathing at Baxters*, RCA 4545; *Volunteers*, RCA 4238; *Hot Tuna*, RCA 4353; *Electric Hot Tuna*, RCA 4550.

**Rick Danko**

Plays with the Band; can rock when he wants and play soft slow tunes with ease. Sometimes uses a fretless bass. *The Band*, CAP STAO 132; *Stage Fright*, CAP SW 425; *Rock of Ages*, 2-CAP SAB 11045; *Northern Lights/ Southern Cross*, CAP ST 11440.

**John Deacon**

Bassist for Queen. He plays in the hard-rock tradition with a fine group. *A Night at the Opera*, ELK 1053; *A Day at the Races*, ELK 1091.

**John Entwistle**

Plays with The Who. One of the world's foremost rock bassists, he always has inventive bass lines. *My Generation*, MCA 4068; *Happy Jack*, MCA 4067; *Sell Out*, MCA 4067; *Tommy*, MCA 10004; *Smash Your Head Against the Wall*, MCA 2024; *Whistle/Rhymes*, DL 7-9190.

**Andy Fraser**

Played with the rock group Free; has an imaginative rhythm-and-blues style. *Fire and Water*, A&M 4268; *Best of Free*, A&M 3663.

**Tony Levin**

One of New York's top session bassists, and deservedly so. He displays a few styles on this record. *Peter Gabriel*, ATCO 36-147.

**Paul McCartney**

What need be said? Anything by the Beatles or Wings.

**Felix Pappilardi**

Bassist and producer for Mountain, a hard-rock group. *Avalanche*, COL 33088; *Best of Mountain*, COL 32079.

**Carl Radle**

A leading West Coast session bassist. Any Leon Russell or early Joe Cocker.

**Michael Rutherford**

Uses his bass as a melodic instrument with this English classical rock group. Any album by Genesis.

**Chris Squire**

Anyone who can play bass this well and sing at the same time is just fabulous. Any Yes album.

**Willie Weeks**

A session bassist with some very funky rock lines. *George Harrison 33 1/3*, Dark Horse 3005.

# Riffs and Chords for Guitar

### Blues Riffs for Guitar
### by Mark Michaels

This exciting new compendium gives you hundreds of riffs in the styles of all the major blues masters. By playing and using these riffs, the blues player can gain important insights into the theory and, more important, the feel of the music; how performers like Freddie King, Albert King, Buddy Guy, Otis Rush, Eric Clapton, Mike Bloomfield, and others get that true blues emotion into their playing. Useful for beginners as well as professionals. Chord changes for all riffs are included, plus performing hints and a discography. In standard notation and tablature.

### Rock Riffs for Guitar
### by Mark Michaels

This unique "how-to-build-riffs" approach for the electric guitar includes musical excerpts in the styles of Chuck Berry, Jeff Beck, Duane Allman and others. Special sections cover picking, fingering, bending, muting and hammering. Single and chordal riffs are all graded from easy to advanced. Discography included.

### Jazz Riffs for Bass
### by Rick Laird

This exciting new book, written by the former bassist with the Mahavishnu Orchestra, teaches the intermediate to advanced player how to develop a fluent solo technique. The acoustic or electric bass player can learn to play riffs in the styles of Eddie Gomez, Scott La Faro, Ron Carter, Stanley Clarke, Jaco Pastorius and others. Jazz scales and modes, odd time signatures and modern techniques are all covered in depth. Also includes solos, notes on practicing, a convenient chord scale chart, a bibliography and discography.

### Rock Riffs for Bass
### by Tom Wolk

This book offers a wealth of material for the electric bass player who wants to learn to play in the styles of Paul McCartney, Jerry Jemmott, Harvey Brooks, Chuck Rainey, Rick Danko, Phil Lesh, Jack Bruce and other great rock players. Styles covered range from rock's early beginnings to the most modern synthesizer-type bass lines. The riffs are built on authentic rock progressions, and include New Orleans, Memphis, Motown, disco, pop and reggae music. All pieces show chord changes and fingerings. Discography included.

Available at your local music store
or directly from:
Amsco Music Publishing Company,
Dept. BA, 799 Broadway,
10003 N.Y.
New York, U.S.A.